Happy Christmas

Promise to spread love & joy

S Afrose

Ukiyoto Publishing

All global publishing rights are held by

Ukiyoto Publishing

Published in 2023

Content Copyright © S Afrose

ISBN 9789360491994
*All rights reserved.
No part of this publication may be reproduced, transmitted, or stored in a retrieval system, in any form by any means, electronic, mechanical, photocopying, recording or otherwise, without the prior permission of the publisher.*

The moral rights of the authors have been asserted.

This is a work of fiction. Names, characters, businesses, places, events, locales, and incidents are either the products of the author's imagination or used in a fictitious manner. Any resemblance to actual persons, living or dead, or actual events is purely coincidental.

This book is sold subject to the condition that it shall not by way of trade or otherwise, be lent, resold, hired out or otherwise circulated, without the publisher's prior consent, in any form of binding or cover other than that in which it is published.

www.ukiyoto.com

Dedication

Respected Muhammed Zafar Iqbal

Muhammed Zafar Iqbal is a Bangladeshi science fiction author, physicist, academic, activist and former professor of computer science and engineering and former head of the department of Electrical and Electronic Engineering at Shahjalal University of Science and Technology.

I am the lover of his books, especially the science fiction. Those books are incredible. I have learnt so many things from those canvases. So beautiful and lovely. Just, wow!

I didn't meet with him, in person. But it's a sign of my love, towards his paradise. Dear Sir, hope you will be happy, taking my love, without any hesitation.

"Love & Respect"

Acknowledgement

Thanks a lot Dear Almighty for blessing me always.
Thank you so much dear parents, friends, readers, well wishers.

Without yours' supports, I can't be able to walk smoothy onward.

Thanks a lot dear Ukiyoto Publishing Platform, for loving my words, as the canvas of writes.

I am so much grateful to this wonderful planet of poetry. This is my paradise. My soothing charm, to make any rhyme. How wonderful!

When mind loses its spirit to rise up, poetry helps me to be strong enough, to hold the lost motion of the life.

Again Thank You so much dear Almighty, for being my best friend forever.

© S Afrose, BD. 16th Dec-23.

Happy Christmas

The beautiful cart! It is coming here from the sky.
So wonderful. The snowflakes' vibes! Everywhere
can see the whitish fairies of dreamy earth,
covering by the snowballs' kites. Really?

Can't believe. How could you say?

On that cart, someone sits joyfully, with a smiley
face. Wow! Who is there?

The Well-wisher, The Angel, from heaven to
earth. Oh! Really?

Hearing so good. The cart stops. That person
comes out. There's a bell-Jingle bell. It is ringing
all the way. Below, so many children with elder
ones. They make the sound –it's Santa Clause, Yes!
He is here. He has bought so many gifts for all.
Come on and accept this part.

"Take this promise today-

Spread love and joy

Towards the universe.

Share and care,
Happy Christmas!"

Tomorrow will be the new sunshine.
No more tears & fears.

Happy Christmas... a poetry book, reflects the core messages about Christmas Ray.

For example- **Dear Day, Christmas! Christmas! Come Back To The Dreamy Life etc.**

Hope you will get some special essences of this poetic flower.

(For any kind of unexpected words, just forgive)

Thanks!
From Author Desk ♥
© S Afrose, BD. 16th Dec-23.

Contents

Christmas Day	1
Dear Day	3
Christmas! Christmas!	5
Mysterious Train	7
Christmas Lane	9
Christmas Tree	11
Come Back To The Dreamy Life	13
That Poor Child	16
The Melancholy	18
The Gift	20
The Time Is Too Short	22
Time To Say, He Will Be Dear.	25
Christmas	27
The Magic Tree	29
Over There	31
The Snowman	34
The Suitcase	36
Close Those Eyes & Make The Wish	38
Your Thoughts	39
Violin On The Way	40

Children With Beautiful Dresses	42
On The Table	44
Nostalgic Moments	46
Broken Foundation	48
Open The Door	50
Thinking And Writing	52
Midst The Ocean Of Feelings	54
Passion	55
Stop	56
Variant Dots	58
The Newspaper	60
Wheels Of Life	62
Best Time	64
Don't Mind	66
Snow Mountain	68
Key	70
Golden Wishes	72
Significance of Christmas	74
About the Author	80

Christmas Day

Christmas! Dear Christmas!
How are you?
Where are you?

We are waiting
For your arrival,
The whole year.

Oh dear Christmas!
Come on and show us,
Which is essential for this time.

Happy Christmas

You are
The Magical Flower,
For this universe.

(4th Dec-23)

Dear Day

Waiting and waiting, we are here.
When will arrive, dear Santa- Christmas.
Everything decorates as per love,
Children say- we love your arts.

Santa is already made the mind,
Buying so many gifts and gifts,
Everything is full of love,
Lots of dreams cover by heart.

Each gift provides this unique essence,
Hold the hands forgetting any pain.
If you want to enjoy life,
Need to shower love and love.

Christmas tells this story,
Christmas shows this vibe.

If you want to smile,
You have to believe this part.

Dear Day!
Christmas ray!
Everything prays
Christmas ray!

(4th Dec-23)

Christmas! Christmas!

Christmas! Christmas!
Merry Christmas!
Come on dear all-
Look at that ride.

Santa Clause! Dear Santa!
Giving his mystic smile,
He has a lot of gifts.
Come on and hold this time.

What is in your mind?
Tiny wishes?
You can find that,
In that box of gifts.

The essence of love-
The precious treasure,

Happy Christmas

Don't act as a loser.
Christmas is your best supporter.

You can learn from Santa.
How can spread fragrances of love?
How can make the merriness hub?
Christmas! Christmas!

Sweet smile!
Christmas! Christmas!
Adorable heart,
Touching us.

Christmas! Christmas!
A great surprise,
It's our pride,
To make the eternal hut.

(25th Dec-21)

Mysterious Train

What an auspicious time!
The trailer of movie
Is running,
Showing
So many incidents.

Clear, not at all.
Clear, not clear.

It seems like a train
So many compartments,
A lane,
Which contains good and bad, so many trails.
Equally swaying.

Look at the mysterious train.
It takes my desires in the distant lane.

Happy Christmas

I'm worried about your existence.
Can you wait for a moment?
Some new aspirations.

Clear, not at all.
Clear, not clear.

Those aspirations,
Making a troll.
Why don't see?
Life rolls and sings,
Let's make this ride on this mysterious train.

(4th Dec-23)

Christmas Lane

That lane
Looks,
So different.

The core point!
Who knows?
What is the meaning of that green?

An old man!
Grey bearded,
With a smile.

Known as
The magician,
For this lane.

What's that?

Christmas lane.
Christmas is coming.

That man
Prays,
For the happy earth.

This is the gist overall.
Christmas comes only once.
Need to hold this motion forever.

(5th Dec-23)

Christmas Tree

A tree!
Hopefully
The dreamy cage.

It is decorated,
With so many lights
And the stars.

The great news!
The green plant!
The sparkling planet of our hearts.

The glory of Christmas!
Rock and roll, not optimal.
Open the eyes of heart.

Santa Clause and you,

Happy Christmas

Magical vibe overall,
Just love and respect.

(5th Dec-23)

Come Back To The Dreamy Life

Never make this
So fussy,
So miserable.
So sorry,
Solicitude of life.

Come back to the dreamy life!
Come back to the dreamy life!

You know that,
Once was.
Most welcome.
Now count me in,
Not welcome.

What?

Why?

Come back to the dreamy life!
Come back to the dreamy life!

Look at there,
Your garland of fears.
Block the tour of mind.
Can't escape?
You don't aware.
Surprised?
It's just a shocking vibe.

You know, what?
Look at the yard,
The desired tree of your life.
Christmas peeps.
Comes to you
From so far,
After a long longing thirst.

So dear,
Come back to the dreamy life!
Come back to the dreamy life!

(5th Dec-23)

That Poor Child

He lives
With his mother.
So poor.
Just a shabby attire.
Still, he enjoys

He says,
Christmas will be here very soon.
Mom!
What will I get from the Santa?
What will be the blooming gift of my life?

This is the chord of Christmas.
Lots of wishes and love,
Shower love and love,
Over all of us.

The pool of water
So cold,
Still it looks so happy;
As the Christmas is here very soon.

That will show
The warmth touch,
To make
A pool of cheerful mind.

Mom says!
My dear,
Definitely
You will get the best gift,
From the Santa.

This Christmas is the blessing,
For all of us.

(5th Dec-23)

The Melancholy

Today is so special,
For me, not.
As you are not here,
My dear sweet Mom.

Today is the joyful night,
For me the melancholy verse.
As you are not here,
Once you were its heart.

Today is Christmas.
Holy moment, Holy arts.
Holy sense, mingled mind.
Today, without you, ah!

Christmas! Dear Christmas!
Can't you make this?

Once again,
Make the day so hilarious.

The Melancholy!
Not for me.
I want to smile,
Give me back that, dear.

(5th Dec-23)

The Gift

Waiting for that sound.
When will hear,
The tune of bell,
Jingle bell.

This is most acceptable.
Something will appear,
With desired hope and love.
The Holy Christmas!

At last the cart,
Snowflakes ride,
Meadow of heart,
Happy Christmas!

Clarify your thoughts.
Nothing can be stopped,

When hear the ringtone,
Jingle bell, all along.

A little cart,
Fantastic bard,
Happy Christmas!
Dear Earth.

(5th Dec-23)

The Time Is Too Short

The evening!
Very shortly,
It turns
Into the flowing dreams.
With glowing lights
Of Christmas Trees.

Chill!
So beautiful.
Then-
Mind says
The time is too short.
It will go away
Very soon,
From our huts.

Oh no!

Children cry.
They say,
We want Christmas,
Every time.

The Tree says-
Look at me dear,
I am here,
To bestow
My love and friendship.
You will nourish this
All the time
Over your life.

I will take my Farewell,
And will wait,
To meet with you again;
To know,
How could you accomplish,
My signs?

Happy Christmas

The time is too short
For this time.

Bye! Bye!

(5th Dec-23)

Time To Say, He Will Be Dear.

This is not right to stop.
Time, you say to all,
Hello! My dear earth!
Hello! My dear people.

All of you are so special,
Little to older, not a matter.
I know you know we know it.
Christmas, the magnamious gift.

As our next day comes,
Will flow and glow with sweet rhymes.
World asks, what?
We will say, Happy Christmas!

That is the sign of happiness.

Need to accept and spread.
Christmas is the blessing part,
Hello dear! Accept and love!

Time to say, this moment,
Hello!
Dear!
My sweet love!

My Paradise,
My gems of life.
Time to say, he will be dear.
He is the Christmas Peer.

(4th Dec-23)

Christmas

Christmas! Christmas!
After a long time
It has come as a new sunshine.

It sparks in all hearts.
Spreads fragrance of happiness.
Shows way of hope,
Showers love for all.

Hello dear universe!
Here is the magician.
Santa Clause with his rider,
Ready to make the dreamy ride.
He will knock at each door,
To give each one his mystic box.

That box will hold the gift,
To see to know, how do you think?

When you will see the ray of love,
You may realise the meaning of life.

Christmas! Christmas!
Merry Christmas for dear all.

(25th Dec-22)

The Magic Tree

That's the magic tree.
Midst the yard,
Midst the hut.

The tree
Of love and dreams,
That is the Christmas tree.

Everything is free.
When you see,
Your heart flies.

That beats
For all,
For the desired universe.

Happy Christmas

The magic tree!
Makes us free,
From all the hostile glees.

Host this time.
Making your heart,
Sincerely for the song of life.

(5th Dec-23)

Over There

The cart
With the deer or horses
Who will say?

It comes
From the sky,
On this earth.

The snowy time!
The snowy night!
All over the whistle of winter.

Winter comes,
Snowy weather.
No care.

The cart is here
Full of joy,
A person is there.

He is dear Santa,
Coming to all
With a big backpack.

Full of gifts
Joy and joy,
No falling snowballs.
This will make
The single space,
For us.

Hello dear!
Really amazing,
When can see that cart.

(5th Dec-23)

The Snowman

The white shaped doll
Snowball?
Oh!
It's the Snowman.
He is here
With his smile
So beautiful.

Wearing the black hat
A muse, that's the fact.
The long shaped nose as the carrot dances.

The fallen winter
Tries to kill us,
But the Snowman loves us.

Showing
The bay of life,
So beautiful, onward.

(6th Dec-23)

The Suitcase

She holds the handle
Of that suitcase.

The long way
Not familiar.

She thinks
Is that right to be there?

Still time to think
How can go?

But can't stop
As need to find out the desired destination.

Recall the past
The Snowman's smile.

Along the cold weather
The sweet cage of life.

Alright
Ready for the ride.

The suitcase!
It will help to hold the hands of mind.

(6th Dec-23)

Close Those Eyes & Make The Wish

Close those eyes
To see
What do you like?
Close those eyes
To make the wish
Once was in the mind's ward.

Make your wish.
How can you want to see,
Your desired life?
Don't forget dear,
Santa says this always,
This is the time to live happily
With all.

(6th Dec-23)

Your Thoughts

Bizarre plot!
Your thoughts.

Hold this nut
You have the gut.

You knew that
Nothing is false.

Along with mind
Thoughts, flowing chime.

(6th Dec-23)

Violin On The Way

The Violin!
On your way.

You played
And enjoyed.

The song
From the deepest heart.

It says
Merry Christmas! Merry Christmas!

Take this again and play.
Spread each note of the song.

Christmas gives this chance.
You have to optimize this port.

(6th Dec-23)

Children With Beautiful Dresses

Come on children
Take these dresses,
These are only for all of you.
You must love, at a glance.

Such a kind hearted person,
Too much essential,
Ripping out all the rifts.

Children enjoy the time.
They love
Holding hands as the friends.

They will be the leaders of future earth,
They have to realize this part,
They will make the beautiful waves of life,
For that dreamy universe.

(6th Dec-23)

On The Table

The red cloth
Covers the table.
On that place
A beautiful gift.
People sit
On the chairs.

Those are so familiar
For this time,
Will you come?
Most Welcome.

Let's have a drink,
Smirking!
Hope it's the sign of positivity,
It will restore the lost smile.

(16th Dec-23)

Nostalgic Moments

Is that sight, my turn?
Nostalgic mind for a moment.

Nostalgic Moments!

Once
The world,
The Paradise,
All the time.

Nostalgic Earth for this time.

Oh no!
Not like this word.
Kindly hold this one.

We are here
With the nostalgic moments,
For restoring the paradise.

(16th Dec-23)

Broken Foundation

Inside the room
A newborn.

He or She
The song of life.

Upside
The dark sky.

Nobody is here
Who will care?

Broken foundation of earth
Uncertain.

Christmas tells the story
Broken foundation should be resolved.

Gradually hold
Play the friendly role.

(16th Dec-23)

Open The Door

Go ahead.
A closed door.
Open the door.
Pls, open the door.

The door opens.
A smokey vibe.

Floating sky!
Wow!

Call, all the people.
We are dear friends,
We will be always.

Don't forget your step
Is ahead.

Open the door.
Pls, open the door.

(16th Dec-23)

Thinking And Writing

The aged one
He is.
Lonely?
Not at all.

He is with the friends
Of nostalgic past.
He adores
He loves.

The opened diary!
The black pen!
The ink!

Yellowish pages.
Sober!
Nostalgic happiness.

Desires, where?
Lost the mind
Once again.

The aged man,
Angry at a glance.
Should I?

Thinking and Writing
On the pages of life
Finally.

A clue
Anew,
This moment.

(16th Dec-23)

Midst The Ocean Of Feelings

Searching all the sites
Melody of life.

Midst the ocean of feelings
The tune of life.

In depth
What's that?

Lost melody.
It looks as your dear.

Note this part,
You will be able to feel this art.

 (16th Dec-23)

Passion

Passion!
When life losing its vision.

Passion!
When mind wants its junction.

Should recall,
When the way is in the amazed jinx.

A second,
Know this option.

Passion
For the proper equation.

(16th Dec-23)

Stop

This is the sign of hand.
Stop.

Why?
Clarify.

Ahead may be hostile,
You have to prepare, dear mind.

Stop
And think.

You made the wrong deed.
Right?

May be.
It's time to survive.

(16th Dec-23)

Variant Dots

Full the box
Variant dots.

Multiple rules
Give an easy clause.

Pause!
A pair of notes.

Your choice.
There's the exam board.

Take the chalk.
What is in your mind?

Variant dots,
Be the boss.

(16th Dec-23)

The Newspaper

The news is all over.
Merry Christmas!
Merry day of life!
Merry earth!

The newspaper!
Dances as the butterfly.

The butterfly!
Comes from the eternal hub.

The hub!
Full of sweet vibes.

Love it.
Nourish it.

The newspaper!
Your best art for this time.

(16th Dec-23)

Wheels Of Life

The red sky.
Why doesn't it look as the bluish one?
Who will give this answer?
I want to know this of course, dear.

Wheels of life!
Wheels of life!

The life's car.
Uncontrolled.
The break fails
Oh my dear Almighty!

Need to concentrate
To make the proper connection,
For the better earth
Of all.

Hello dear!
Come on
And say,
Is that right or wrong?

I know,
It's not an easy answer.
As the life is on the way,
But wheels may be collapsed, any time.

(16th Dec-23)

Best Time

Hearing the song of mind.
The best time.
Yes it's true,
For this year
Christmas, the best time.

So many balls
So many balloons.
So many gifts
So many children,
So many people.

Best time!
Together
They sing the song of mind.
The best time
Of the dearest life.

(6th Dec-23)

Don't Mind

If anyone tells,
You go to the hell,
Pls don't mind.

As you know
Your dreamy slot,
Deepest the mind.

You can get
At any trace,
Believe in heart.

Forgetting rifts,
Making the shift
Of nonsense words.

The whole earth
Your desired mart.
Yes dear bard.

(16th Dec-23)

Snow Mountain

Snow falls
Always.

A Mountain
Rises.

Is that the ghost?
Oh My God!

Mountain moves
To all.

Play with your dearest doll
Sweet baby.

As the Christmas's season,
Snow Mountain is all over.

(16th Dec-23)

Key

It's just a key.
The favourite key.
You left behind
And lost the map of crucial movements.

Keep quiet.
Remember.

That key
Can unlock the door of mind.

It asks-
Keep me in your love.

Don't lose ever.
Then locked the mind.

(16th Dec-23)

Golden Wishes

Cover
The rest.

Here
The chest of dreams.

Golden wishes!
Golden wishes!

Holy Day!
Christmas's Bay!

People enjoy,
Golden ray.

Christmas, so meaningful,
When mind makes the divine pool,
Full of golden wishes.

(16th Dec-23)

Significance of Christmas

In the whole year, those people are waiting for something very special. Children wait for the desired lane of happiness. What's that?

Christmas! Happy Christmas!
Christmas! Happy Christmas!

Children tell: Mommy! Mommy!
Oh Daddy! Oh Daddy!
When will come that Christmas?
We want to see something very special, want to get many beautiful gifts from dear Santa.

Daddy: Pls tell us the actual time. We can't wait anymore.

Parents: Dear Children. Our sweet arts.

Don't worry. It will arrive very soon, with all dreamy gifts.

"Hey you. I will arrive very soon. Be ready to welcome me."

Be ready to share your lovely thoughts, happiness with all. No segregated parts. Be the part of all the lovely hearts.

You don't know,

CHRISTMAS TELLS US-

"Happiness is the crucial part of our lives. Sharing and caring, the prominent parts, my dear world."

Oh!

How sweet!

We will wait.

We will make this in real term...

The desired time. Most popular sound can hear from so far. Jingle bells!

Dear Santa has come with so many gifts.

Gifts for you, I ... gifts for all the people.

> **"Come on dear Children.**
> **Here, your gifts.**
> **Hold your breath.**
> **Spread love.**
> **Don't break any heart.**
> **Know and know...**
> **Share your love with all"**

What a melody of this song! What a melody of this heart!

The sweet song is heard. Lalalalala...

> **"Be my friend**
> **Be my love**
> **Be my heart**
> **Be my lovely art"**

The beautiful word. Love and love.

Foe or friend?

What's that?

I can't understand. Oh my dear Santa! Pls tell me the legend of this Glittering Art.

Dear Santa comes.

Dear Santa asks all the children.

Hey dear all, Listen.

You know, what? We all want to live, showering petals of love. This is essential for the sweet universe. But look at this part, we don't see the ray of the golden sun. That sun is the heart, to resurrect the soulful vibes of the earth.

It's possible by all of you, dear Children.

Christmas comes to spread this message-hold all hands by singing the song of the dreamy life:

Spread the lovely gifts.

Spread the lovely mind.

Spread the fragrance of the lovely arts.

Santa holds the breath and distributes the surprised gifts to all.

Not only for the children but also for the people of this universe.

"Santa tells- we have the power to restore our paradise. We must accept this motto. We must spread this fragrance, as the flying birds of the Sweet Earth."

Copyright © S Afrose, Bangladesh.

14th Nov-23

About the Author

S Afrose

Author S Afrose (Sabiha Afrose, from Bangladesh) has made her writing realm since August-2020.

She enjoys each of the part of this writing ward. She tries to express the hidden word or emotion, by her words; with the glamour of poetry. Poetry is her best friend. Her writes have been publishing on magazines and anthologies (90+). In this writing realm, she has achieved many awards (beyond her expectations eg. Doctorate in Literature from Instituto Cultural Colombiano, Literoma Laureate Winner 2022, Mahatma Gandhi Award 2023 from Instituto Cultural Colombiano, One of the World Record Holders for Hyperpoem, etc.)

Published author of poetry books- **Thanks Dear God, Poetic Essence, Reflection of Mind, Glittering Hopes, Angels Smile, Tiny Garden of Words, Dancing Alphabet, Artistic Muse,**

Essence of love, The Magical Quill, Dear Children, Haunted Site. Woman, The Butterfly, A Little Fantasy, Lion's Roar, The Bride, No War, Lost Lotus, Friendship.

All are available worldwide (on Amazon.com & from publication hub and from other sites-Flipkart, Bookshop, Booksgoogle, Barnesandnobles etc. also, as any format). Apart these, there are some Bengali and English poetry books (available on rokomari.com in Bangladesh).

Her mother is Selina Begum and father is Manirul Islam.

Educational achievements- B Pharm, M Pharm from Jahangirnagar University, Bangladesh.

Hobbies are reading, writing, specially the paradise of the poetic flowers.

Contact- afrosewritings@outlook.com, sabiha_pharma@yahoo.com

You Tube: S Afrose *Muse of Writes*(@safrose_poetic_arts)

Facebook page: Muse of Words by S Afrose

Twitter:@afrose2020

Inst. @safrosepoetryworld

**"THANK YOU SO MUCH
FOR BEING MY DEAR,
WITHOUT ANY FEAR
MY DEAR POETRY WORLD"**

www.ingramcontent.com/pod-product-compliance
Lightning Source LLC
LaVergne TN
LVHW041537070526
838199LV00046B/1711